15-Minute Market Research for Affiliates

How to Make Quick Money with Affiliate Marketing by Finding Untapped, Low Competition Niches You Can Take Over Right Out of the Gate

By reading this document, the reader agrees that under no circumstances is the author responsible for any losses, direct or indirect, that are incurred as a result of the use of information contained within this document, including, but not limited to, errors, omissions, or inaccuracies.

Table of Contents

Introduction

Do you ever wonder why some affiliate marketers do so well, while others seem to be left in the dust?

It isn't some magical lucky break they have; it's the market they choose to use, and the niches they decide to go into. These decisions make all the difference between whether you're successful or you fail as a marketing affiliate.

In this book, we'll tell you the secrets of affiliate marketing, and how to do market research quickly and effectively.

The Research is Where It's AT!

Research is how you become the best affiliate marketer out there. You should also make sure you're willing to make the marketing content necessary to succeed. If you're doing it for a market that's not super popular it can be hard. Luckily, in this book we understand the importance of research, and we'll tell you how to do it fast.

That's right. It's that simple. If you do research, you'll have a successful niche.

Some do believe that you need to do hours and hours of research just to get the right niche. But you don't. You can do so in about 15 minutes.

You read that correctly. In just 15 minutes, you'll have the perfect marketing research campaign in place, and you'll know exactly how to move forward from there.

Here, we'll highlight the easiest way to find the right niche in just a few minutes, and also how to do it through various sites. We'll also tell you about some free and high-quality market research products to try out.

Don't spend hours and hours slaving away at the computer just to find one niche that *might* work. Instead, work smart and do the research quickly; so, you're able to get the most out of your marketing as possible. You need to know what the right niche is and what to do to be successful within it. Even if you have experience in market research, this book will help you to drive your affiliate marketing even more!

We'll make the job easy and in only a few minutes we'll show you how you can be the best affiliate marketer out there.

Chapter 1: How to Find the Right Niches for Affiliate Marketing

Figuring out the right niches for your product marketing is a bit harder than you think. Lots of people just choose whatever market they can find, but there is an exact means to figuring out the right affiliate market for you to work in most successfully. In this book, we'll tell you of the easiest ways to find the right affiliate market, so you feel better and more satisfied with the work you're doing.

Find One That Fits Your Brand

Some marketers think just going into health, wealth, and romance is the way to do it. But that isn't the case. The right way to conduct affiliate marketing research is to look for the niche that fits your brand.

The best way to do it is to figure out which niches are best for your brand, and what it is you want to write about. Affiliate marketers who put their sites together with affiliate pages that fit their brand do a lot better than those who just choose the affiliate product based on something that's popular.

Understand It's More Than Just Trying to

Sell a Product and Hoping for the Best

Many who begin with affiliate marketing think that it's easy income because they don't have to do anything.

That's where they got it wrong.

The big thing to remember here is for those who are interested in affiliate marketing, they have to put the right program in place. You shouldn't just think it's merely providing links and inbound tactics; it's more than that. You don't just sit on your butt and relax. In fact, most CMOs who do this will tell you that effective affiliate marketing is one of the skills people tend to brush off. Most people don't get the sales and conversions they need, because they don't put the effort in.

The truth is, only a few people get the majority of these profits, and it's tough to be one of those few. Some affiliate marketers struggle because they don't choose a niche that fits their brand, or the niche isn't one they're willing to market.

Research is the biggest thing about affiliate marketing. It's what really matters. If you fit the research to what you want to do with your brand, you'll succeed.

Don't Be Afraid to Get Detailed

Of course, you don't want to be too detailed, but do consider more specialized markets. For example, you can consider cruelty-free products as an alternative to regular products. Cruelty-free is a much smaller market, and it also isn't so niche people aren't looking for it. People want cruelty-free products, so you can work with that. There is a smaller group of people that purchase these, and it's easier to market yourself in this market than going against the regular common products. Plus, it's a hot topic, so people will buy this type of product, since there are fewer sellers of this niche.

If you're still not thinking about getting detailed, then you should reconsider. While yes, selling skin creams on your beauty website is great, but if they can't be marketed to a niche audience, it won't work.

Another tactic that goes with the previous one, is to look at the top 100 sites in one industry, or even just the top 100 in general (Patel, n.d.).

You don't want to copy the sites, or try to fully emulate the industry, since you're not going to be noticed that way. You will be dust in the wind if you do so. You want to go to the third page of the top websites, where they become more and more niche. For example, if you go to the third page, you will see more niche blog websites, and that of course, will hit a narrower target than you would with say, eBay or even Walmart's website.

You'll notice that once you do this, you'll have a good idea for a niche industry. However, you need to make sure to narrow it down even further. Travel is incredibly popular, yes, but that's super broad for affiliate marketing. From there, you can go to Quora and type in some of the top questions that in the search site, and from there, narrow this down and develop smaller niches. For example, let's say that you have cat products. doing just generic cat product information won't get you anywhere. What about different cat products your furry friend will love? Or even the hottest toys and some of the fun ways to use them?

Writing affiliate products for this niche, such as cat trees or even cat treats will help you. The end goal of this is to create smaller niches within each sector or industry. Cat care hacks are incredibly popular, and you can from there, move to more specific or weird cat care hacks that you feel will fit your brand best.

This is a great way to narrow it down. Never try to start with a broad niche against the big guns; it won't get you anywhere.

Consider How Evergreen the Niche Is

What does evergreen mean? Well, it essentially means that it's a niche that will always be popular for you to sell in.

For example, being an affiliate for the newest Galaxy phones might not be a good choice because the phones will eventually reduce in demand. Phones get a new model every single year, so unless you are going to be on top of all Galaxy phone news and are prepared to remarket with each new phone it might not be the most painless affiliate choice you can make.

Another topical example is bumper stickers, namely political bumper stickers. They probably only work for the term of presidency. Unless it is for vintage purposes or adjusted to fit the current political climate, selling outdated bumper stickers will make your content seem tacky. If you're trying to sell Bush stickers in the current year your audience will wonder which cave you've been living in and have less respect for your site and other products. The same goes for some of those products that went out of style ten years ago. MP3 players aren't as necessary these days since our phones do everything.

Seasons and holidays can be difficult as a niche. Ugly Christmas sweaters don't sell year-round. Similarly, Halloween costumes might be hugely popular for a few weeks, but after Halloween is over, so is the hype.

In order to make affiliate marketing work, you need to make sure that your niche and products are popular year-round and thus marketable year-round. The best way to find out if your niche is evergreen is to use Google Trends, set up the keywords, and from there, determine how popular it is, and whether or not there is growth or potential for growth. For example, keto diet foods are popular for the most part and have had pretty steady growth, since it seems like everyone is doing keto these days. While it's true, fad diets do die out over a while, they're still a profitable niche market in general. A good proportion of the population will be turning to some sort of diet product to help with losing weight at some point in their lives.

The same goes for skincare items. People are always thinking about their skin and how to make it better. The niche itself is very strong, but even more, some products within the niche have proven to be seemingly eternal. Proactiv for example is still incredibly popular in the skin care world, despite being on the market for over a decade!

The concept of a product or niche being evergreen is essential for you to understand if you want to succeed at affiliate marketing. If you grasp the concept and are able to identify products and niches and whether they are evergreen or not, you are well on your way to making it big.

Of course, it is important to check and see if the niche is growing. But it is almost more important (in my opinion) to determine its evergreen status. Many fads can result in a niche growing dramatically within a short period of time; but not every niche or product can stand the test of time and be marketable for years. If you find one of these evergreen niches, treasure it!

Do You Like the Niche?

A niche has to be something that you like and that you're willing to write content for. It isn't always exclusively about profits; it's also sometimes about whether or not you actually want your brand associated with that niche.

Some of us wouldn't like to write about detox teas for hours, and that's totally valid. There are thousands of niches out there, just waiting to be discovered and marketed. Why would you waste your time on a niche that makes you miserable and takes extra energy to motivate you to work with? If you dislike it, you'll probably feel like you're slogging through a mud every time you attempt to make content, market, or research for it.

It's quite simple. If you're motivated, it'll be easier for you. The best way to do it, is to choose niches you know you like. You will be able to more easily write content that your audience will like, which is incredibly helpful for those looking to market their products on their site.

On the other hand, sometimes you might like the niche but not be especially motivated to write content for that niche. If this is the case, you can stick with the niche, but write content that is similar enough to be considered sub niche content. It is important to understand that you'll always have more than one option and your motivations will fluctuate throughout the process. The more ideas you have and the more flexible you can be, the more options you will give yourself.

What if you are interested in too much? If you have hundreds of niches and you can't decide you need to direct your enthusiasm towards your research to determine which of your interests deserve your affiliate marketing focus. You will probably want to see which niche will get more results over another. We'll talk more about how to do that with ClickBank in later sections, but the quality of your research is going to influence the quality of your results—regardless of how motivated you are!

That said, should you be uncertain or not too happy with any of your options, ClickBank is going to make your life a whole lot easier. The numbers can help you make your decisions for you. We will discuss how in Chapter 3.

Chapter 2: Need a Niche? How to Find Product Niches on Amazon in Minutes!

Amazon Affiliate is one of the best ways to start with affiliate marketing. If you're trying to build an affiliate business, Amazon Associates might the affiliate marketing program to begin with. Amazon Associates, or The Amazon Affiliate program, is perfect for those that already have content or a blog but can be developed parallel to you creating your website as well.

Amazon, as you know, has products in many industries and sectors. It is so far reaching that at least a few products, but more probably thousands, will no doubt match the niche(s) you have chosen. Some new users assume it will be hard to figure out, but this is far from the truth. There is a way for you start earning very quickly, possibly in as little as minutes.

In this book, we'll teach you the niche research skills you need to find the best products and start raking in your commissions. We'll give you a quick and dirty step-by-step guide to help you navigate the niche market and determine which products to add to your affiliate website. We will also show you how to do the research quickly so you're not mulling around wasting your time.

When Choosing a Niche

When choosing a niche, there are a few things that you need to look at on Amazon before you begin, and they are as follows:

- How popular it is
- Whether it fits the dynamic of your site
- Whether people are buying it

A lot of affiliate marketers will jump right in and sell any old product, but here's the reality of it: if you don't look at these three criteria, you won't get anywhere.

Once the niche is figured out, you want to start small with a product, and then go out bigger. This takes out all of the people that are too big for you to compete with, but also lets you expand your horizons so that you're getting more and more from this too (Palit, 2019).

You want to make sure that with your product, you're able to make some decent profit margins as well. One of the best ways to do it is to make sure that it is making you at least 15% minimally, so if you have a lot of a product sold, you're making a lot more over time (Palit, 2019).

Most of the stress you run into when choosing your niche comes from whether or not it's high competition or low competition. High competition is not the best choice, because it is a very popular already, and it is probably an oversaturated market. Medium competition is decent, but it still requires significant investment. A lot of affiliate marketers who start with medium competition will notice that they will have to pay for a lot more just to get a leg in the industry.

Lower competition ones are your best bet, and the less competition the better. They're available because either they have not yet been discovered by the bigger players or the earning potential is too small for the big guys' efforts. The bigger guns usually consider "lower amounts" to be something like a grand a month, which might suck to them, but for beginners, that's a decent chunk of change. You should try to rank in the lower competition niches and then scale to other product categories in order to increase the earnings at hand.

The Criteria to Consider

Now that we've narrowed down what it is that you need to focus on in order to choose a niche, go through the niches that you're interested in and make sure a few basic things are true:

- You can rank in the niche.
- You'll get decent cash from being an affiliate.
- It's got subcategories for you to create enough content.
- You have some interest in it; you won't get too bored with it.
- It's not too hype-based or temporary, such as the newest iPhone.
- It doesn't have a lot of recalls, requiring edits to the site content.
- It isn't seasonal, since seasonal items won't get you decent earnings most of the time (SellerApp, n.d.).

If the above statements are true for you, then you're well on your way. Now that you have your niche planned, you can move to the next step: product categories.

All About That Category!

The category you choose will help you fully analyze the competition and determine how much overall work you need to do in the long run.

You can manually browse the different categories and sub-categories and choose accordingly. When you choose a product, there are certain criteria that you should keep in mind (Palit, 2019):

- The average customer rating is at least 3.5.
- They cost at least 50 dollars.
- There are at least 500 monthly searches for it in a product category.
- Two of the products are in the top 1000 in the biggest category, and you can look at the site ranks in your product description (Palit, 2019).

You can also browse sitemaps that specialize in this, and from there, you can build niche ideas in this fashion. While you still get ideas about the broader category of products, you can then narrow them down the sub-niches under the border niches and rank for those as well.

SEMRush is another one that lets you get some ideas. You can use simple filters, with keywords that start with "best" when you apply it, so you're not wasting your time going through all of the unimportant pages (Palit, 2019).

Analyze Your Competition

Look At how many are selling in this niche. Is it a lot? If it is, it might be too taxing to fit into this saturated field. You can also check the keyword to see the competitiveness of it, which is something we'll discuss later. You should do this because it allows for you to check through hundreds of different keywords in a manual manner (AMZ Finder, 2018).

When you do this, you might find some niche sites that sit at the top three, and while they might not have the domain, dofollow links, or authority, they rank well. That's because they're using the private blog network links that are hidden from your common crawlers, so they can't be seen. You should check the link profiles of the pages ranking using Ahrefs, since that has a much larger and fresher dataset than the others, and it will show whether or not it's an authority site. This in turn will help you figure out which Amazon niche sites are in place that are hard to take over.

Affiliate programs will have certain types of products that you can add to your site, and once you've found the right products, you can from there, find the right affiliate networks to work with. Make sure your affiliate network has this item or different items listed that you can add for content on your site, and make sure that you measure the different affiliate products with how they rank on Amazon and how profitable they are. Look at the competition of the products the niche sites that you have too.

Understanding what your competition looks like is one of the most important aspects of this. It is very simple, and very effective.

You can from there try to calculate how much money it will cost to be an affiliate for the niche. You might not make that estimate the first month, but it's at least a guide to determine potential.

Check Customer Reviews

When setting up your affiliate marketing site, you should check customer reviews. This also gives you a keywords tool. Do you ever look in the corner and see those little keywords added and wonder what they are used for?

They are actually the main keywords people use when discussing the product. For example, you might see "great for running" for a pair of trail running shoes at the top, and that's because lots of people are saying they're great for running.

What's amazing is that you can build an entire page based off looking at just those words. By saying "What are the best shoes that are great for running," you can note the readers' discussions, and from there generate a page of content. You simply add in the affiliate links, and there you have it.

Customer reviews are a great way to figure out the right types of keywords to add, but don't forget to check the competition to see if they'll rank, and whether or not they're something that is actively sought out (AMZ Finder, 2018).

Will This Really Take Five Minutes?

The answer is yes!

Read below for the summarized step-by-step summary guide on how to discover the best affiliate products on Amazon.

1. First, you choose a niche you like or feel passionate about. Scan at the products within that niche, have a look at how popular it is, and ask yourself if it is an evergreen niche.
2. Next, look for specific products related to that niche that are currently available for purchase. Note whether or not they're selling and how much you can make from each purchase.
3. Next, do keyword research so that you can get a good look at the state of your competition.
4. From there, if you find a niche that's doable and you determine you can make decent profit margins from, then you can follow the instructions on Amazon to set up and join the affiliate program.
5. Once that's completed, you can build your website if you don't already have one.
6. Create content that you can insert the affiliate product links naturally into.
7. Use keywords from the different parts of the products and the main keywords from reviews in order to build content that'll cover all of your bases.
8. Consider using the "best ____ for __" template when building content for the site.
9. Check your site to make sure it ranks.
10. Net those profits and build your affiliate product catalog along the way.

That's all there is to it! It doesn't take long to do any of these steps. Just take it one step at a time. You'll be selling affiliate products through Amazon in no time at all.

Chapter 3: How to Easily Find ClickBank Niches

ClickBank is a way to figure out the monetization of the niche you've chosen. It is also one of the best ways to figure out the right niche to work in, since it has a lot of amazing digital products that you can use, is super easy to navigate, and it has the "gravity" filter, which tells you what is and isn't selling.

In general, a gravity of at least 6 is what you want, since that means it's a sellable category. Later we'll discuss how you can figure out how to find the right topics that sell well and how to eliminate those that don't (ClickBank, n.d.).

Go to Categories

First you want to go to the 'marketplace,' and then choose 'categories,' which will show all of the categories that are available on the site on the left-hand side of this site.

You can also go directly to the affiliate marketplace and then choose a category from the drop-down menu. The lists in this case are already put together and rightfully curated.

Once you do this, you click on the categories to see all of the subcategories that you can look into.

The best thing to do here is as well to make sure that you filter out the categories to things that are selling and things that are interesting and relatively relevant to the niche you're putting together. The more interested you are in something, the more motivated you are to do the content for this site.

Let's take for example the health and fitness category, which is a popular one.

When you do look at this, you're likely to find 200+ different results. That's a lot, and once you start to filter it, you'll notice that it will still have hundreds of options. The best way to go forward is to trim the fat, in a sense. It's setting you can use so that you filter out the products that aren't selling (Fylan, 2015).

How to Trim the Fat

So how do you trim the fat and filter results? The answer is to go to the gravity. You can manually set this to 6, and it'll eliminate anything that's under a 6, which means it isn't selling well. Or you can set it from high to low, which essentially will show the best affiliate products to the worst ones (Maina, 2017).

From there, you want to look at the products that you feel will be easy for you to sell quite readily.

Look at the gravity that's there, how much you'll get out of it, and the categories add the average per sale. I highly suggest going for an average sale of at least 60% or higher, a gravity over 6, and something that's pretty popular, but still keeps you from dealing with too much competition. This is a very easy way to look at the niches and find the services and products people want to pay money for.

When you start trimming this, you should still see a lot of products. You might notice that the niche that you wanted to sell in has no gravity, in which case you should continue to look around applying the same filtering techniques.

Look to Find the Best Options

Don't just settle for the first thing you get. You should look through some of the different keywords that are there. You'll want to hunt through this in order to find the products with a gravity of 6 or more, and things that might not be in the right category, since they might be under health, or even under different topics (Aversity, 2018).

You don't have to spend too long at the beginning, especially if you find your niche right away. But you can still go further and look for similar products that might be hiding within the search box.

If you're pressed for time, go with the niche that best fits your site, and then compare the keywords on AdWords to see if it has potential to make a sale. Ideally, you're willing to put in a little more time, so you can take keywords within the product and look for the different relevant products. You should also look at the quantity and frequency of these products' sales. If you notice some certain keywords shave your results to less than 10 products with a 6 or more in gravity, it's best to move on to another niche and look for something else. If you stick with so few results and available products, it'll be harder for you to make the niche worth your while (Maina, 2017).

Look at the Sales Pages

If you've done a lot of research already and you feel like you need to still dig a bit deeper, then off to the sales pages you go! This is a good way for you to fully understand the niche topic and the products that are available within that topic.

A thorough and deep understanding is important, because some products might come up during your research, yet be very unrelated to your niche. For example, sometimes you might see "detox" used not for fit teas, but rather for kicking out toxic people from your life. Sure, that might be good for a mental health and wellness blog, but it's not so useful if you're trying to hit the weight loss market.

You can from there find at least 10 pages and products that are relevant to this, and you should make sure that you're using only relevant items related to the keyword that you want to go with (Affilorama, n.d.).

Don't try to use those other products that make no sense for your niche and instead, work on the niche in a relevant way that will help you net a profit.

Take your time with this

With this you can surely find a niche in a quick and painless way. It might be a little bit more frustrating if you're someone that had a specific niche in mind and were really set on going forward with that niche. Ultimately, if you discover through the ClickBank research that it is not as lucrative as you hoped, it's still better to cut your losses and move on to another more valuable niche.

With that in mind, don't get discouraged if it takes a few minutes (or longer) to find the right niche. It is very important for you to figure it out properly in the beginning to ensure you reap benefits in the long run. I promise it will all be worth the effort!

Let's look at another example. Take selling luggage for example. That niche in itself is too broad for you to do, unless it happens to be some weird, innovative, ergonomic luggage. You might be thinking, "But I don't know the first thing about ergonomic luggage!" At this point, don't worry so much about whether or not you have an idea of how to sell it, but instead, work on going through the steps to pinpoint the best niche on the market.

When making your decision, you should minimally accept 40% commission when starting out. Keep in mind that ClickBank will take out transaction fees during the sale, which is why we encourage you to you calculate how much you'll be getting from it before you choose a service to focus on and work with (Maina, 2017).

As an affiliate you will need to disclose the links that you're using as well as making sure that you mark these as a nofollow. The reason you need to do this is because the nofollow means that webmasters, bloggers, and web publishers can put these links in, and make sure to not count the links as a vote up. If you don't have that as the tag, the search engines will then opt for the pages that are linked to quality sites that will take the link without compensation. Marking this prevents your links from looking like spam, especially since larger sites involving affiliate marketing gets thousands of these a day, so you'll want to make sure you follow the correct procedure.

What Next?

We have already learned a lot about ClickBank, but there's more! Below are a few additional bits of information to further support your ClickBank experience.

The first step is an important reminder: to choose the products you'd like to promote and link to. Now you know that you should obviously promote products that you think fit your niche, but also remember to choose products that you would actually consider buying yourself or that are something that you personally find interesting. Believing in the product will make you better at promotion, since you'll have an authentic understanding of what will draw the customers to the product you're listing. By promoting products that you feel passionate about, you'll surely stand out from the others!

The affiliate pages on ClickBank also have tools and tips available. They include guidance on how products should be promoted, the images and keywords that work, and a whole lot more. You should always check the keywords, but the other aspects of this source are worth looking at as well.

Don't forget to monitor your HopLinks and campaigns. They are things that you should check and test to ensure they're in proper form and working right.

You want to make sure that while yes, you do the research, but you also use the right promotional means to get the information and the deals out there. You'll need a wide array of promotional techniques to help you begin with this.

Also, the best affiliate marketers are flexible with the techniques that are there. Understand that what might have worked for you in the past might not work now. Even stuff that worked a year ago might not work very well today. You should make sure that you understand that affiliate marketing is something that is and will continue to change rapidly, so you should be ready to adjust to the new trends, products, and changes every step along the way.

After you've done all the research and the hard work identifying a niche and entering the affiliate marketing world, you'd hate if it was all snatched away from you. That's why it is crucial for you to read, understand, and follow all of the specific terms and conditions of the site that you're using for the product. This goes for any and all sites that you're using in your affiliate marketing. Failure to follow the terms and conditions may be more than a slap on the wrist; they might terminate your account! Many have made this and paid the price of terminated accounts. Don't be one of the sorry ones.

You don't like getting spammed. No one does. So why would you think it will magically work for your affiliate marketing? Be sure that you don't spam too much, or at all if possible. Yes, it does happen sometimes, and it's something that customers continue to complain about. Keeping your customers happy is only one reason why you should limit your spamming techniques. Another reason is you can get banned from many different locales and groups if enough people report your behavior.

Along the same lines as spamming, is negative advertising. No one really likes it; so why do we continue to do it? Why expend the extra energy cutting someone else down when you could be screaming your product's strengths from the mountain tops? It's better for you to write content that highlights why your product is good, rather than just talking smack about how someone else's product is bad.

Through this chapter you've seen and certainly are convinced that ClickBank is probably one of the best places to put your content up in. We highlighted how to do it in minutes and why doing so really works and is worth it for affiliate marketers.

Chapter 4: How to Find a Hot Niche in OfferVault in Minutes!

ClickBank is great, but there are more ways to find your perfect niche. OfferVault is definitely one of those places for you to find hot niches, for example. It's a great way for you to get the market research you need done and done fast. In this chapter, we'll tell you why you should use it and provide a step-by-step guide to using OfferVault so you can keep up with the trends in the easiest way possible.

What is OfferVault?

Before we start using it, let's figure out what OfferVault actually is. OfferVault is a way for you to look up different affiliate programs that fit whatever niche is on your mind. The focus of OfferVault is on the CPA of the affiliate offers that are there.

What this means is, when you send leads and get customer information, you get a bit of money from this. OfferVault can sometimes be considered easier to use when compared to other programs because it doesn't require you to actually make sales.

Sounds too good to be true, doesn't it? Well, don't think you can just do anything (or nothing). With OfferVault, you also have to make sure that you look into whether or not the niche your operating with is a profitable one. This is *very* important. Most go into OfferVault thinking that they have to just choose any old niche, but now you know better. Even if you've chosen a niche, you still need to look further at the results of the niche and confirm whether or not it will get you the profits you desire.

You should understand that not all the niches on OfferVault are good with CPA types of affiliate marketing. Some that you might not be familiar with may not be even listed here. If you see proof of some of the other networks in place, you can look at OfferVault, and from there determine whether the CPA marketing is worth it.

Factors to consider with each campaign

On OfferVault, there are a few factors that can help you figure out whether or not a campaign is relevant. They include:

- the payout
- the network
- the category
- the last time it was updated

Every time you search for different items, you will see the range of offers available. From that list, you can determine what the best offers are and how they compare to similar offers using the factors above.

OfferVault does require some flat, monthly fees from every affiliate network that lists on there. This is because there are a lot of affiliates that search for new networks. This is a great deal for pretty much everyone, and once you start with OfferVault, you can always join other networks, or send traffic to this site and others. This approach is great for creating leads, and you'll get a commission from each sale from the network. You simply choose the program that you want, and the process is very simple.

The Best Types of Affiliate Marketers for OfferVault

Who will benefit from these types of affiliate programs? The answer is pretty much anyone who is willing to put in the time and effort, but here are a few sorts of people that stand to benefit the most from this program:

- Those just starting out as well as experienced affiliate marketers who aren't using OfferVault yet
- People looking for new affiliate tools to help with keyword research and demographics
- Bloggers
- Affiliates looking for different offers for comparison
- Advertisers and online businesses

OfferVault makes it pretty easy to start with affiliate marketing and through it you can find loads of different networks that you can work as an affiliate for. It's also got some of the highest payouts among these types of sites. There is a lot of research material and landing pages on OfferVault. It's very easy to do market research based on what you need and there are constant updates on any new offers that you have.

First Thing's First: Know the Types

One thing that's a bit different about OfferVault is that you can get different types of offers from their site. In this section, we'll highlight each of these offers.

First, you have mobile offers, which essentially means you're getting customers via mobile devices. You can use iPhone and smartphone applications to send these offers, which can then go to sites with different advertisements for promotion. You will want to opt for this type of offer if you've got mobile traffic and mobile tools.

Another offer is called pay-per-call, which is similar to PPC advertising, but this one is done by a payment to the person in the form of a call and not a click. Phone marketing is still popular, and some great publishers continue to get a lot of results from using phone calls.

Then there are the email address and zip code offers. Usually this is a CPA program that offers a free item or a gift card. From these, you get some commission and also can relax knowing the free gift incentive is in line with the rules. You can earn some decent cash through this offer over time.

Finally, you have the new and featured offers. The former discusses the newest and hottest offers out there; and the latter, includes offers that are chosen by OfferVault themselves, such as traffic, offers, banners, and network listings.

The Process of Using OfferVault

The process of market research using OfferVault is quite simple. You can do a basic search, where you simply put in the keyword of the item that you're looking to sell, look at the relevant offers, and from there, look to see whether or not there are any traffic hurdles and whether it's a viable network.

This is pretty different from other approaches, since you'll need to make sure that you look into the different profitable niches that are out there. Your search box is going to be one of your best friends, whether you're looking for eBay offers, Amazon offers, or any other offers.

Simply look for the product, and from there all of the different networks that will have this offer for the merchants can be viewed. True, it might seem difficult to figure out the best one, but your decision is made a bit easier by looking at the payout column. This lets you decide on whether you'll get a decent income and whether it will have profit potential based on the niche. A good rule of thumb is to make sure it is about $10.00 per payout per lead at least in order to make it a decent offer for you.

Tips for basic searches

Basic searches are pretty, well, *basic.* That said, if you take the time to understand the different benefits of a basic search, you can still get loads out of them.

The CPA network that's on OfferVault might even pay you more money than others, so when you're looking at OfferVault, always check to see which one gives you the most profit.

Also, make sure that the keywords you're putting in get you results. Be sure you're getting relevant and appropriate results, since the results are refined, and the search engine captures it.

When you find an offer, note the special instructions that are there. Sometimes, this offer is only available in a select few countries or for limited campaigns. If you don't read the fine print, you might get flagged as spam. You will see all the special instructions, as well as a description, when you click on the offer field.

Finally, if you notice that a page looks a bit more professional, there is a chance that it'll have better conversion rates, so always make sure that you go through every detail while looking at the offer pages.

The Advanced Search

Are you not getting the offers that you want with a basic search? Well, it's time to use the advanced search. For those who want to get into the niches a bit deeper and involve a bit more energy, the advanced search will help you by further refining the search to identify the right CPA to promote.

The advanced search function has several different important aspects to it. We'll highlight each of the useful areas in the following section.

First, you have the keyword in the title, and this is pretty much exactly what it sounds like. You simply put the keyword within the title. Using this function, you can find the exact offer that you're looking for based on its name.

The keyword in the description is pretty much the same idea, but you refine the search based on the results that you find within the description of the offer instead of within the title. Once you get to the landing page preview, you will see the description of the offer.

Next, you have the network search. If you know about networks or know of a specific CPA network that you want to use, you'll most likely prefer this search. This search is especially useful if you have a particular network that you want to invest in or one you want to get a particular offer from. An advanced search of the network will let you find the best product to promote along with finding the right income from every merchant. Currently, there are over a hundred or so of these and they're continuously being added.

There is also a category search. This search is good if you know whether or not what you're looking after is in a certain category. This search is very useful for those areas that are harder to associate with and maneuver into when marketing. The category search is great because it provides a range of different offers that you might want and segregates them into categories, giving you everything you need in order to choose what best fits you. This also works because it provides easy access to offers on niche websites, which helps you become familiar with and find opportunities with those areas you're not totally familiar with.

You might also want to try the allowed traffic search, which lets you allow traffic from different sources. This is a wonderful feature, and great for merchants who won't allow certain visitors, since they might harm the site itself. Facebook, Twitter, and other social media sites are usually not encouraged, since they're considered spam. The allowed traffic search is also good for eliminating solo ad traffic, or brand-name bidding.

You can also search by country restrictions, which might be useful if you work in a different country or want to promote in a certain region. After searching, you can figure out from there whether or not the merchant will accept or not.

Moving on to payout searches, which are based on the type of payout that you want to have. It can be based on clicks, leads, and some of the offers that you feel work.

You also can determine this based on the payout range you prefer. If you have a specific product that you feel will pay you more for than others, this search is perfect. You also can choose a specific maximum and minimum payout that you want to generate from the offers, based on the criteria offered. This is a way to make sure you're turning the highest profits and income with the least amount of work.

The payout search is major, especially if you're looking at all of the different factors of a campaign. Most people don't realize that by looking at the range of payout you are optimizing your time and money.

Advanced searches will save you a boatload of time, and they're wonderful to do if you're someone who knows exactly what they want. So, invest the extra couple minutes into these additional searches and see what it can do!

From here, once you've chosen the offers that you feel will work best for you, you should follow the same routine as before, wherein you check the keywords, make sure that they're popular, and make sure that your research is thorough.

I like OfferVault the most when I know exactly what type of niche I want to work with. However, for some of the other specific niches, it can be much harder to get into, since they tend to be more product focused than anything else.

Chapter 5: Free Marketing Tools Any Affiliate Can Use (Including Free Keyword Research Tools)!

Effective affiliate marketing is done with the right tools, and in this chapter, we'll highlight the best free tools for affiliate marketers. As a bonus, we will also review some of the best keyword research tools out there.

RankTracker

This is a great keyword research tool that uses the Google Keyword Planner, Google Analytics, and the Search Console, along with other methods in order to provide realistic and accurate keyword results. You'll get a series of long-tails, collect the keywords to the niche, and get insights on the search trends. You'll have word combinations and different variants, and you can from there also look at what competitors are using. It's super comprehensive, and it even can tell you the different factors based on the searches, the difficulty of a keyword, your cost per click, the expected clicks from every ad, and so much more. There is also the keyword sandbox feature, which lets you store, group, or even tag and filter the keywords in some way. However, this is only for the desktop, so you may not benefit from this if you're someone who wants to collaborate more than anything.

AdMobiSpy

This is one of the best tools for mobile intelligence and keyword research for mobile markets. It is great for looking for the newer campaigns to utilize, and essentially, it finds the profitable strategies that you need to apply to the campaigns in order to improve conversions and the CTR. The more data that's available to you, the better the ROI success. From here, you can calculate all of the predicted results available and also avoid the strategies that won't work for the business.

For affiliate marketers, this is a great thing to use because it tracks a lot of the networks within the industry, and the interface is very familiar to those push ad spy tools, but it's a better, more high-quality version that allows you to get full feedback on the creativity that you need for your ad campaign. You can get up to four ad networks in two countries and five daily requests, which isn't a ton, but it's worth it (Alshevskaya, 2019).

Canva

Canva is a great tool for those looking for the best website design. WordPress is good too, since it offers great themes, features, editing, and design, and from there you can integrate everything. But no affiliate will do well without the right design, and Canva lets you do a whole lot more, so it's worth checking out as well.

Google Keyword Planner

This is probably the best keyword research tool that's out there, and it works for PPC campaigns and keywords research. Every keyword suggestion also comes with wonderful parameters, such as the average searches done monthly, your competition, the bid flow (whether it's high or low), and of course, the metrics therein.

You can also look at historical data, and from there, filter out the keywords to include or exclude. Then you can add them to an advertising platform if you're running a Google ads campaign or a .CSV report with all the keywords and stats.

There is no exact search volume data on there as you only get a rough estimate. But you can get precise numbers if you run the Google ads campaign. There is a limit to the keyword suggestions too. You can only get up to 2000 different keywords, but this is still a pretty hefty number in itself and it lets you get a lot of keywords directly from their database (Barysevich, 2019).

Google Search Console

This tool is wonderful for those who want to have a decent keyword tool, without all their money being spent on it.

It's a great one to source the keywords that are actually being clicked on or searched. You'll love this tool if you want a realistic look at what people are finding. However, some people don't like the research tool called the Performance Report, which talks about the pages that got the most clicks on Google and the queries that caused them because it can be almost too much for some people as it includes impressions, the CTR, and the average metrics of the position.

It does identify something called the opportunity keywords, which are some keywords that will tell others about you and can help you markedly boost the rankings on your site.

Once you've assessed all this data, it will then be filtered by the devices, pages, and the dates. The tool might not be ideal for those who want the precise numbers, due to the fact that the Search Console will limit the rounds of the states that it shows to the users. If you want some access to your keyword data, you should combine the search console with the analytics. It is a great Google tool, and lets you look at the images, videos, and websites, with the added bonus of a user-friendly interface.

Google Trends

This isn't the traditional research tool that most people use, but affiliate marketers can definitely benefit from it. It will show the popularity of what you're looking at based on a search query, and you'll be able to find the volume of each search of these queries. They usually have a range from 0 to 100, and from there, it will give you insights on the trends, and the interest that others have on the topic at hand. It's further supported by information on the monthly searches of specific keywords over time (Barysevich, 2019). Google Trends also lets you compare the keywords based on popularity, and from there, you can see the queries that are on the rise, and the top keywords. With this information you can analyze the interaction that each query has in a specific area and eventually eliminate whatever doesn't work. It also looks at how the keywords and trends will affect you during the current season in order to refine and better your marketing strategy.

With Google Trends, you can see the top and the hottest keywords that are used for your type of research, as well as the popular trends.

The one downside is that it is not ideal for specific queries. That's because it only looks at popularity, which might suffice in the beginning. But since it isn't designed to analyze the keywords fully like the other types of keywords research tools that are out there, you may find yourself longing after a more thorough keywords research tool over time. Overall, this is a good tool if you simply want to see how an affiliate program will perform and its potential.

WPX Hosting

For new affiliates who need good WordPress hosting, you should use WPX. This has built-in, free support, and it's super easy to get started with.

This service lets you set up with a domain that's reliable and reputable. It is a reliable tool that lets you transfer and put up the domain name. It also offers blocking the private protection, customer support, SSL certification, and of course ICANN Accreditation. WPX has been around for a long time, it's got a wonderful track record, and did I mention it's free?

GTMetrix

Sites don't perform well without having a speedy and responsible performance. Speed and performance, no doubt, will affect your affiliate program. You can decide whether it will affect your marketing in a good or bad way. Affiliate marketing isn't some magically generated system, but rather you have to implement many different aspects of it, especially if you're looking to create traffic, and keep people coming back.

GT Metrix can help with all of that. It will test your site, and from there, you can see whether or not there is a lag in the images and videos that are showing up, and also whether or not there is a lag for repeated users of your site. This will tell you what needs optimizing and what you should focus on. This will also affect the way people use your site right from the start, so make sure you run this test initially.

Compressor

If you're noticing that your website has a lot of laggy images and pages, you need to start optimizing. Compressor is a free tool that speeds up the loading time of the pages without affecting your quality. This ties into marketing because if your website is slow, it will affect the crawlability of the site, which in turn will affect your website ranking on Google, so it should not be ignored.

Heatmap

Heatmap is a free interaction program that's wonderful for those who come to your site often. It is a way for visitors to interact directly with your website, giving you instant feedback.

This is a great tool because not every site is perfect, and you and your site can always do better. This tool will help you improve the experience that you provide for the people who come to your site, and therefore improve the retention rate of the site itself. It will tell you of any feedback that'll benefit you, and best of all, it's free.

It provides real-time analytics based on what keywords are jumping out at people, and what people consider to be hot topics, and from there, you can generate content and affiliate tools accordingly.

BeMob

This is another (somewhat) free service and it has so much to offer. If you want a way to track all of the campaigns that are out there, it will help you with the analyzing and optimization aspects of that. There is a free plan that's pretty decent and offers a lot of great marketing tools, but you can get some paid plans that are a bit more sophisticated with their campaigning and optimization. These paid plans start at as little as $25 a month. If you're looking to splurge, and can justify this, there are plans for up to $499 a month. That said, the free version is pretty easy to work with and offers some wonderful campaigning items (Sherer, 2018).

SEMRush

SEMRush is another one of those "free" tools, as it has a small trial period before payment is required. If you try it out and it works for you, it is definitely a worthwhile investment. This is great for looking at the competitors of your PPC campaigns. It's a competitive research tool for paid campaigns and one that is incredibly hard to beat. This one lets you analyze the competitors' keywords and budgets, monitor the ad copy and landing pages, discover the new competitors within your ads, and also localize the ad campaigns. There is also a CPC map, which lets you optimize the spending on certain locations.

This is wonderful for affiliate marketers since it makes putting together new ad copy or split testing the campaign super easy. Furthermore, it provides you with organic search results for every single keyword, giving you that extra edge over competitors. You can also look for keywords that even the top competitors didn't realize were there. SEMRush will find the low competition keywords as well as the ones in high demand. This along with the keyword difficulty tool and ad history can make you a winner in the affiliate marketing world.

Jaaxy

Finally, we have Jaaxy, which is an application that makes your keyword research a whole lot easier and lets you collect a lot of keywords while you're at it. It combines everything from Bing, Google, and Yahoo, and it also gives you data for comprehensive keyword research. Jaaxy creates a lot of SEO metrics on every single keyword, such as the quoted search results, which will tell you how many other websites will try to rank for search queries. It also offers the SEO metric, which will estimate the likeliness of ranking on the first page based on your competition and traffic. After the tool has created a bunch of new keywords, you can focus on the ones that are the most profitable by making a simple keyword list. Jaaxy is wonderful, but it is pretty limited since there are limited searches, and the keywords in the free version don't come with opportunities for filtering. That said, it's still a decent addition to your marketing arsenal, especially for those beginner SEOs. Additionally, Jaaxy offers extensive keyword data, smart metrics for keyword analysis and comparison, lists of keywords, tutorials, and it has a mobile-friendly interface, an intuitive design, and helpful customer support.

You might wonder if you should potentially invest in these services. That is ultimately up to you and your specific situation. It's your marketing, your affiliate research, and your choice.

Chapter 6: How to Find Untapped Low Competition/High Demand Niches

Despite what you might think, there are untapped markets that don't have a lot of competition and are still in high demand. But how (and where) in the world does one find them? Read on to find out the secrets of how to discover these markets.

Media Tools

Media, whether it be social media, news, or publications, is actually really helpful for finding untouched niche markets. Simply looking at the news will tell you of new trends that are happening, and you can further narrow down any trends from there. Magazines and articles will keep you informed about what people are interested in, and in some cases, quite simply obsessing over. When you note these, as before, see if there are any niches within the content that you can tap into. From there, you can start to find different affiliate programs.

There are many ways to use social media to investigate and research niche markets. You are probably already familiar with some platforms and procedures, but perhaps haven't used Pinterest to improve your affiliate marketing and find untapped niches.

You can start by simply typing in your idea or interest, for example, 'travel.' Travel on its own is much too broad. But immediately upon typing it in the search, you will see many sub-topics in colored tabs below it. For example: (travel) quotes, (travel) destinations, (travel) accessories. These are essentially niches. But don't worry, you can get even more specific (and potentially untapped/high demand). Let's click on one of those tabs, say accessories. You will instantly see *even more* subtabs, further narrowing the new search of travel accessories. From here you might decide that luxury travel accessories are the most lucrative, interesting, and relevant topic for your niche marketing--and you got to that decision through some light social media surfing!

Uber Suggest

This is a type of keyword research that involves recommendations based on keywords. It allows you to reverse engineer the SEO of competitors, improving the state of your current content marketing and social media marketing. You can look at suggestions and strategies that others are using, and use them, too! Discovering them and implementing them will make sure you stay in the game.

You can also look at the top SEO pages with this service in order to see what trending searches online are saying. You can look at competitor rankings with this too and figure out where your niches stand and if it's worth it to tap into these types of markets.

Look at Trends and Searches

The next place to look is at Twitter hashtags and Google Trends. You can look at Twitter hashtags to touch on the here-and-now of your affiliate marketing. This is how you tap into super niche markets but do understand that you must act on your research quickly.

That said, these searches are not always inherently good for identifying niche markets. You can at least look for phrases in order to figure out whether or not to move forward with an idea.

With trends, obviously look at the ones that are relevant for your niche. Let's say you're trying to sell makeup products that are cruelty-free. You can highlight the benefits of them, how celebrities are getting involved, and so on.

Put that in Google Trends, and from there, you can get even more subtopics leading to even more niche topics to discuss and also providing a look into what others are saying about it. Some people like to use Google Trends, but in actuality you can use any trend searching tool to see what everyone's talking about and curate content from there.

Niche-Specific News

There is more to search engines than just typing in keywords. You should always go to the news and check out the press releases on the search topic. You can even set up alerts to come to your email so you're aware of any updates or conversations that might pop up about your niche. This will prepare you to adjust your marketing or tap into new submarkets according to the news cycle.

You should also look for and stay up to date on information about company changes, procedures, problems, and potential failures. When companies do fail, their old customers have probably gone after a new source to supply their demands. There are usually reasons for company's going down, such as not managing money correctly, or being too slow to adopt. If you identify these instances, you subsequently now know this is might be a niche market that you can look into.

Ahrefs

Ahrefs is a paid service that allows for you to analyze the competitors, research keywords, backlinks and content, track ranks, and monitor websites. It also provides an organic report on searches, in which your customers will rank an organic search and the traffic that's driven by them. The top pages will help you to see which have the most site traffic. There is also a content gap that's used to help with uncovering keywords that may rank for you. You'll be able to use this site to see what your competition is doing, or possibly not doing. If they're not touching certain niche keywords and content, get in there and do it yourself!

Good Ol' Wikipedia

Did you know Wikipedia can help you find niche markets as an affiliate marketer? Here's how you do it. The simple way is to go to the site itself, and from there put the niche that you'd like to work with straight into the search bar. You'll immediately see relevant results. Within those results there are always highlighted keywords or subtopics relating to the niche. You will not only get ideas for new relevant niches, but you also now have the information to help you build your related, affiliated content.

It sounds easy enough, but you still need to put in a bit of effort. Wikipedia doesn't automatically give you a ready-made list of keywords and niches, but it does give you everything you need in order to figure out the niches.

Use PLR for Niches

PLR, or public label rights content, is usually known for being junk, and for good reason. Most of the stuff you find on PLR tends to be really bad, and not written with sale in mind. However, if you're looking for research on sub-niches, PLR can help. You can go to any PLR site, and on the right side of the page you'll find many different categories of different PLRs out there. A lot of them are targeted, but some of them also have sub-niches when you click on them. You can use these as fodder to build your affiliate marketing content. It is still part of the niche product and doesn't involve too much work to get the job done.

Once you have that, you can go to niche blogs and take some of the ideas that they use, making sure to make them your own. Don't simply copy and paste, because this will only make things worse. You should always make sure that the content is 100% your own, or Google will flag your site.

Forum Time!

One way for affiliates to find sub niches or more in-depth, untapped niche content is to go to the forums of pretty much anything you think you might to sell. On forums you'll find the main niches that are out there and then a bunch of sub-niches that come along with that subject. You can find these niches by taking a closer look at the subsections of the forum. All of these different sub-sections are essentially viable markets to tap into.

You should look at how popular the topic is and how much discussion it is generating. If you know something is a popular or up-and-coming niche, but isn't yet being discussed all that much, you might want to move in on it.

Look at the Audience Segment

The audience that your competitors are usually focusing on is another place for you to find untapped markets. The audience that your competitors are going for are of course fair game for you too. But, even if you can't win them over, they can still be of benefit to you. Look at the problems the audience has and whether the competitors have noticed the problems and are working to fix them. If they aren't, it's your turn to try.

For example, let's say you're an affiliate for dog toys. Your competitors are focusing on the hottest toys on the market right now. But the audience is discussing their concerns about toy safety. They are also asking for advice on how to personalize the generic toys. Are your competitors addressing that?

Put simply, sometimes you are showing customers what they want and sometimes the customers are showing you. Taking note of audience concerns will help you to open your eyes and ears to what your potential customers are communicating and demanding.

Find That Competition, and Find it Fast

The reality of it is that you have the potential to find these untapped niches daily and you can do it within minutes. But, since this is the case for you, it is also the case for other affiliate marketers. This means you need to stay light on your feet, flexible, and constantly searching for the hottest untapped sub niches. They can change at the drop of a hat, and you don't want to miss out on the party!

Chapter 7: How to Find the Hottest Offers for Your Affiliate Marketing Campaign!

Finally, let's talk offers. There are so many affiliate programs and offers, but not all of them are created equally. Every single one of them has their pros and cons, and you don't want to be duped into getting into the wrong affiliate program for your business. In this chapter, we'll help you find the best affiliate offers, why it matters, and what you need to watch out for.

Why You Need a Good Affiliate Offer

By finding good affiliate programs, you're serving both the audience, and your business. That's because they're never fully guaranteed, and if you're picking the wrong one, you'll realize it's not profitable for you or for anyone. Quite simply, if your audience doesn't like what they're getting, they'll leave, and it'll destroy the trust that they have with you.

The secret to successful affiliates is the trust you build with your demographic, so you want to make sure that you meet the audience's needs by providing high-quality information. You also should make sure you are incorporating affiliate offers that they like and that they'll actually use.

But, how do you do this? Read below to find out.

Affiliate networks are where you want to begin, since they coordinate between the merchants and the affiliate. They take care of the payments to the customers, work on commissions, and pay the affiliates at hand.

As we've said before, ClickBank and OfferVault are two of the best, especially since they're known to be trusted sources.

Picking Your Affiliate Offer

When choosing affiliate offers, you will want to avoid issues as much as you can. The best ones are usually the more well-established networks. Sometimes, they're run in-house, such as with Amazon, and others are third party affiliates. However, there are a few things that you can do in order to ensure that you get the best affiliate offer for you.

First, look to see if the network is stable, or if they have spikes and dips. If the latter is the case, there is a risk that you might not be paid.

You should look at the affiliate payouts too. A simple Google search will tell you the state of this company, whether they're reliable on their payouts, and inform you of any issues people have had previously.

You should also check the terms and conditions. Understand that some terms and conditions mention that you can't work with other companies for the duration of your tenure with the affiliate, so it might be best to choose one that offers some leeway on this.

Additionally, be sure to look at their offers. See if they fit the brand image and if that market is growing. While selling the latest phone might be a valuable affiliate offer at the moment, if you don't see it being profitable after a while, it's not worth investing in.

Now, if you've considered all of these factors and noticed that the affiliate offer fits the criteria, then you're good to go. However, even with your best research, understand that not every offer lasts forever, and sometimes, having multiple affiliate programs is a good idea though it may not be possible in some circumstances, especially newer niche content that might not have much traction as of yet.

There are many affiliate networks which we haven't mentioned yet. There are a few that stand out from the rest and are worth noting.

- CJ Affiliate
- eBay Enterprise
- ShareASale
- Neverblue

All of these networks are pretty effective and easy to use. Though not as popular as the affiliates we've focused on previously, it's good to have as many options as possible.

Other considerations when choosing hot affiliate networks

When you choose your affiliate networks, you should also look at how these offers benefit you based on keywords and whether the items are seasonal. Also, be sure to take note of the categories they offer. These considerations, and the suggestions that follow, should be made *before* you dive in.

First, look at the advertisement quality. Is it a product that you would want to buy as well? Do you feel like this retailer is worth working with? While the offer might be great for some people, if the quality of the product stinks, then it won't be worth your investment.

If you do think that this is something you want to sell, look at the compensation, not just the commission rate. You need to consider the way you're going to get paid, such as the earnings per click, the order values on average, the commissions on average, and also the tracking gap.

You also must consider the reversal rate. Sometimes if customers cancel, you might not get the earnings or commission at the initial rate. If you are working with a company that has high cancel rates, this is a clear indicator that customers aren't happy. If you're working with a company that doesn't have many order cancellations, then it's a sign they're a good company to work with.

Finally, look to see if they offer banner ads or creative ads that work with your site. Some like to use links to promote affiliate content. Banners are a nice touch; however, the problem with some banner ads is they look very jarring and ugly, so if a company features those eye sores, it might not be the best choice.

Be the Client

If you have a niche that you want to work with, you should look deeply into the products you're selling and become familiar with them. Do this with each and every product.

You don't have to use it yourself, but it does help. However, if you're reading over the product and you can't grasp what you're supposed to do with it, this might be a red flag. What people don't understand is that some affiliate programs and offers don't explicitly tell you what their product is in a way that makes sense, and if you can't describe the product you're offering, is it actually worth selling? Not really. If you're looking to make extra money, it really helps to get an idea of what you're working with.

Look at all your offers from the viewpoint of the client. Think like the buyer. Look at the reviews of the product to catch a glimpse of what customers are thinking about the product. For example, I don't think selling snake oil is very valuable since many of the reviews end up being fake and many customers aren't happy with the outcome of their purchase.

Look at Competitors' Affiliates

For some people, even if they're already doing well with one affiliate program, they might wonder what would happen if they branched out to another. Look at the brand or product you're an affiliate for, and then look at competitors. See if they have their own affiliate program.

Some think it's a little unfair cause you might be taking money from the other, but it's not. You're just the affiliate and unless the terms and conditions say otherwise, you should look at both the current affiliate program you're working with and the competitor programs to best optimize your earnings.

Having these additional products within a category or even from direct competitors increases your chances for a conversion. This beneficial as some customers may only buy from a specific retailer and they might shy away from buying from you if you're not an affiliate of their program. It's important to understand that the search for retailers to work with and the search for merchandise are, indeed, one in the same.

Research What Your Audience Wants

Once you've looked through the programs, look at what your target audience is into right now.

For most affiliates, this is done through the keyword research phase, but you should continuously look at the trends, and look at the different hot topics your audience is clamoring on about. This will be important since it will help you stay relevant and up to date on the products you're selling.

Look at the customer profiles, and always keep current on these. You need to look at the type of person that's buying from you and if that is the type of customer you want to deal with. If you already have a customer base, then it's as simple as looking over what customers are buying the most and what type of customer is purchasing from you already.

For example, some people notice that their audience consists of mostly younger people, so they want to work with affiliates that offer products that are ideal for younger audiences. Maybe your top audience is empty nesters. In that case, you should write products and content that will help you lure them in even more.

This also works with finding the hottest offers. You know who your target audience is and what they're interested in the most. So, you can easily go to affiliate programs and look for the offers and programs that fit the vibe of your customer, website, and content.

You already know the importance of research choosing affiliate programs that are known for selling well and are in demand. You can investigate a bit further by using surveys, emails, or even blog posts that encourage people to leave comments so that you can get a feel for their opinions and desires.

When studying your competition social media helps immensely. You can look at what others are struggling with, figure out if your niche solves these problems, and from there, market accordingly.

The Commission Earnings Per Click

At this point, you should probably know of the ideal types of offers you want. If you've already looked through ClickBank, OfferVault, or even Amazon, you might now be curious about the criteria of other sites.

You must look at commission rates and your earnings through click as you are looking at how much the product is selling.

Some believe the commission rate is of sole importance, but that is not the case. It's also the order rate, which is called the average order rate, or AOV. Your AOV tells you straight up how much you're going to make. You will also find out how much you can potentially sell. While something might have a super high commission, if it's not selling, it's not worth it. The same goes for a product that's got a very low commission rate but is selling amazingly. The number of products sold impacts the AOV, so you should look at having one with a higher AOV to start with, and later on perhaps put those higher-commission products on there.

For example, let's say you have two types of shoes. You've got some generic walking shoes, which are selling great, but the commission rate is a little low. In the other corner, you have high-end, expensive weight training shoes, which earn you a hefty commission for each sale, but you're not selling much (Sherer, 2018).

In general, walking shoes will sell a lot more often and you'll earn more money in the long run. So, it isn't just the commission rate you need to look at, it's also if the product is a hot item, if you're competing with a ton of other affiliates, and how much you can potentially earn overall. But that isn't to say that high price products should be avoided at all costs. In the next section, we'll discuss why.

High-End Happiness

Some people prefer the fancier things in life, and that applies to affiliate marketing too. For some affiliates, their audience isn't the average Joe or someone who is looking for the cheapest product that simply does the job for them. Some people want those higher-ticketed items. If your audience is people who want high-end jewelry, you can go ahead and take those luxury products.

There is somewhat of a misconception that luxury items are harder to generate sales from. But, for some people, even just selling a few of them could earn an affiliate a ton in revenue as a result.

Again, this all depends on the type of people you're working with. That's why it's encouraged to be willing to offer a vast range of products, since this will allow you to attract a variety of potential customers.

You still need to make sure that this product is something people want to buy or will solve issues people have. While it might be cool to be an affiliate for a 3,000-dollar dragon sculpture and you earn 300 dollars a commission, there aren't too many people buying that. But, for rich people who have money to spend, they might want to buy the expensive couch rather than something that is cheaper and of lower quality (Sherer, 2018).

Sometimes, you might even have affiliate offers that offer something called a recurring commission which means that if the customer buys from the merchant again, you get a little more. It might not be likely unless this is a disposable product people will need again and again, but it is still something to definitely consider.

Consider Upsell Offers

Finally, consider the upsell offers. Upsells are a way for you to earn more as an affiliate. Once the customer gets their initial product, they are offered other packages that are only available once the item is purchased. For affiliates, if they get a sale from the product and later from the upsells, the commission no doubt becomes higher and higher.

Upselling is especially useful to consider if you have multiple products that can be sold with the original product that you're an affiliate for. For example, if you are promoting laptops, offering an accompanying laptop case would be a perfect upsell opportunity. All in all, upselling opportunities are something to consider and keep in mind when you are deciding which affiliate programs you choose.

Finding the hottest offers takes time, and you should do an in-depth analysis to get the results you want. That is why these little hacks are so important to incorporate.

Conclusion

Affiliate programs are only as successful as you make them.

If you're selling garbage products, you'll likely get garbage turnouts from them. But, if you are an affiliate for offers that fit your brand, that are easy to sell, that are popular and trendy, and that you have numerous keywords, you'll do well.

Keep all of this priceless information in mind the next time you research your products. I know for many people, this does take a chunk of time out of their day, and it isn't the most enjoyable thing to do, but in time you'll see the benefits outweigh the cons.

If you do your research right, and follow the tips this book has given you, you won't actually need to spend copious amounts of time on your affiliate marketing. Now you are able to use your time effectively and work on finding the right products to sell. Even just spending 5 minutes on ClickBank or OfferVault to look for what you need will help you in your journey to becoming the best affiliate you can be.

If you're still unsure of what to be an affiliate for, the simple answer is to do your research, and from there, the products will come to you! Your niche is your power, make it work for you!

References

Fylan, J. (8 Jul 2015). *How to Find the Affiliate offers to Promote.* Retrieved from: https://prettylinks.com/2015/07/how-to-find-affiliate-offers-to-promote/

9 Tips to Find your Amazon Niche Product. Retrieved from: https://www.sellerapp.com/blog/find-amazon-niche/

AMZ Finder. (17 Oct 2018). *What to Sell on Amazon 2019: 7 Steps to Find your Niche Products.* Retrieved from: https://www.amzfinder.com/blog/sell-amazon-7-steps-find-niche-products/

Maina, A. (12 Jan 2017). *How to Use ClickBank Affiliate Marketing: A Step By Step Guide.* Retrieved from: https://smallbiztrends.com/2017/01/clickbank-affiliate-marketing.html

Aversity. (2018). *How to Use clickbank to Make Money Online.* Retrieved from: https://aversity.com/blog/how-to-use-clickbank-to-make-money-online

Affilorama. (n.d.,). 4 Steps to Finding Profitable Affiliate Niches. Retrieved from: https://www.affilorama.com/market-research/choosing-a-topic

Sherer, S. (22 Mar. 2018). *10 Tips for Choosing Affiliate Marketing Programs that Work for You.* Retrieved from: https://www.awin.com/us/how-to-use-awin/affiliate-marketing-programs-that-work

Palit, R. (11 Sept. 2019). *Amazon Affiliate Niche Sites: Step by Step.* Retrieved from: https://techtage.com/amazon-affiliate-niche-site-guide/#tab-con-3https://www.affilorama.com/market-research/choosing-a-topic

Patel, N. *How to Find a Profitable Niche in Affiliate Marketing.* Retrieved from: https://neilpatel.com/blog/find-profitable-niche-affiliate-marketing/

Rito (29 Mar. 2017). *How to Use OfferVault: The Affiliate Marketer's Guide.* Retrieved from: https://www.flyingstartonline.com/offervault/

Affilorama. *How to Find Affiliate Programs.* Retrieved from: https://www.affilorama.com/introduction/how-to-find-affiliate-programs

8 Powerful Hacks to Find Profitable Sub-Niches in Any Market. Retrieved from: https://nichehacks.com/profitable-sub-niches/

Alshevskaya, T. (6 Nov. 2019). *The Best Ad Spy tools For Internet Marketers in 2019.* Retrieved from: https://www.mobidea.com/academy/ad-spy-tools/

Tips for New Affiliates. Retrieved from: https://support.clickbank.com/hc/en-us/articles/220366087-Advice-for-New-Affiliates

Berysevich, A. (20 Mar. 2019). *5 of the Best Keyword Research Tools in 2019.* Retrieved from: https://www.business2community.com/seo/5-of-the-best-free-keyword-research-tools-in-2019-02181286

Sherer, S. (2 Mar. 2019). *The 12 Best Free tools For Affiliate Marketers*. Retrieved from: https://www.awin.com/us/how-to-use-awin/the-12-best-free-tools-for-affiliate-marketers